ThemeWorks™
An Integrated Curriculum for Young Children

At the Seashore

Joan Westley
Illustrated by Elaine Abe

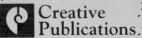

Creative Publications

THEMEWORKS™: AT THE SEASHORE

Creative Publications is a registered trademark.

With special thanks to Betsy Verne Franco and Holly Melton.

Grateful acknowledgement is made to the teachers and children who tried these materials in their classrooms:

Marlene Getz ◆ Berkeley, California
Kathleen Hammer ◆ Mountain View, California
Becky Kenfield ◆ Missoula, Montana
Kathy Muench ◆ Schaumberg, Illinois
Carolyn Nuite ◆ San Francisco, California
Claire Piccinelli ◆ Redway, California
Pearl Seidman ◆ Concord, California

Project Manager: Micaelia Randolph Brummett

Research Editor: Ann Roper
Graphic Designer: JoAnne Hammer
Production Artists: Normajean Franco and Roy Kutsunai

©1991 Creative Publications
1300 Villa Street
Mountain View, CA 94041
Printed U.S.A.
ISBN: 1-56107-081-5

5 6 7 8 9 10. 9 6 5 4

Table of Contents

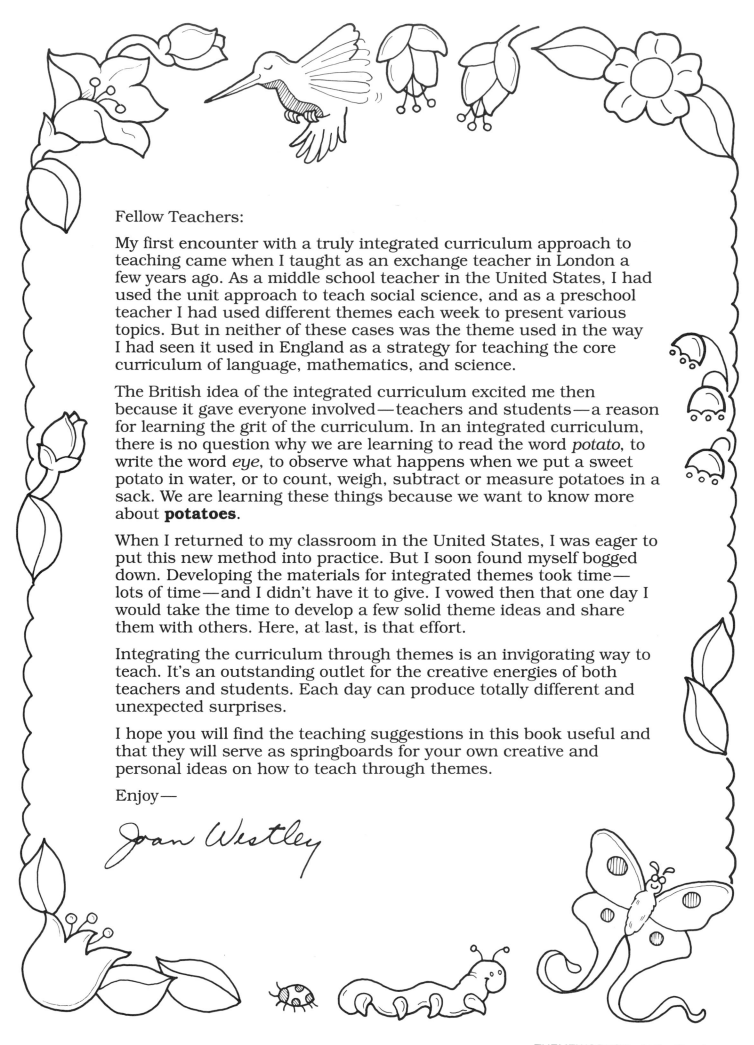

Fellow Teachers:

My first encounter with a truly integrated curriculum approach to teaching came when I taught as an exchange teacher in London a few years ago. As a middle school teacher in the United States, I had used the unit approach to teach social science, and as a preschool teacher I had used different themes each week to present various topics. But in neither of these cases was the theme used in the way I had seen it used in England as a strategy for teaching the core curriculum of language, mathematics, and science.

The British idea of the integrated curriculum excited me then because it gave everyone involved—teachers and students—a reason for learning the grit of the curriculum. In an integrated curriculum, there is no question why we are learning to read the word *potato*, to write the word *eye*, to observe what happens when we put a sweet potato in water, or to count, weigh, subtract or measure potatoes in a sack. We are learning these things because we want to know more about **potatoes**.

When I returned to my classroom in the United States, I was eager to put this new method into practice. But I soon found myself bogged down. Developing the materials for integrated themes took time— lots of time—and I didn't have it to give. I vowed then that one day I would take the time to develop a few solid theme ideas and share them with others. Here, at last, is that effort.

Integrating the curriculum through themes is an invigorating way to teach. It's an outstanding outlet for the creative energies of both teachers and students. Each day can produce totally different and unexpected surprises.

I hope you will find the teaching suggestions in this book useful and that they will serve as springboards for your own creative and personal ideas on how to teach through themes.

Enjoy—

Joan Westley

THEMEWORKS™ : At the Seashore
©1991 Creative Publications

Teaching Notes

What is *ThemeWorks*™ ?

ThemeWorks is a series of teacher resource books created especially for prekindergarten through grade two teachers who wish to use an integrated approach to teaching the curriculum. Each *ThemeWorks* book centers on one powerful theme. As the children investigate the theme, they engage naturally in language, math, science, cooking, poetry, literature, dramatization and art activities. The theme also provides a springboard for large-scale projects, dramatic play centers, and the construction of classroom environments.

ThemeWorks heavily favors the whole language approach to developing language skills. Children are exposed to language through chants, songs, stories, poems, and rhymes. They are encouraged to play with the rhythmic and repetitive structures in rhymes and chants and they begin the process of writing using these frames. Reading is developed through the children's own speaking and writing.

Counting and number work are developed through meaningful problems that evolve out of real situations relevant to the theme. Emphasis is on number concepts and relationships, organizing numerical data, and measurement.

How were the themes chosen?

There are hundreds of possibilities for themes, but the best themes are those that provide the potential for a broad range of activities across all the curriculum areas. We chose themes that were rich sources for songs, poems, storybooks, and rhymes. Also considered was the theme's appropriateness for the developmental levels and interests of young children. The themes addressed in this first series of 64-page books are:

Night Time
Rain
Houses
Trees
At the Seashore
Under the Ground

How is *ThemeWorks*™ organized?

Each theme is organized into three distinct parts:

- the kickoff,
- the theme activities, and
- the culminating event.

We recommend that each class do the kickoff and the culminating event and then pick the activities they would prefer to do in between. This arrangement allows an individual class to make a theme study as personal as possible and to adjust the length of time devoted to a particular theme to meet individual needs.

What is the kickoff?

We begin each theme with a kickoff event related to the theme. For example, the exploration of the night time theme kicks off with a pretend sleepover at school. This activity gives everyone involved a sense of expectation about the theme that is to be studied.

The kickoff is designed to capitalize on what children already know about the topic rather than require any specialized knowledge or skills. It also provides an informal assessment of what students already know about a topic. It starts them focusing their thinking on what they want to learn about the theme.

The theme mascot is also introduced during the kickoff. This mascot is a puppet character that serves to give instructions, introduce new ideas and songs, and provide friendly guidance throughout the theme study.

This is also a good time to begin a theme web and a word bank.

What is a web?

A web is a brainstorming tool and graphic organizer. At the center of the web is the name of the current theme. As children name subtopics of the theme, each idea is connected to the center by lines. Through this brainstorming process, the class begins to see all the avenues of exploration that are available to them through the vehicle of the theme. Work on the web can go on throughout the investigation of the theme. A sample web is shown on page 8.

What is a word bank?

A word bank is a dictionary of words related to the theme. Entries for the word bank may be suggested by the children any time throughout the exploration of the theme. A sample word bank is shown on page 8.

What happens after the kickoff?

Between the opening and culminating events, each *ThemeWorks* resource book offers 18 mini-topics related to the theme at large. Each mini-topic is presented on a two-page spread. By scanning the Table of Contents, a teacher can choose those topics she feels are most appropriate for her class's study of the theme at hand.

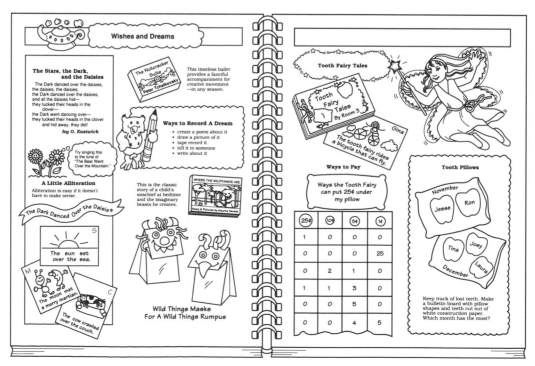

How does the theme exploration end?

At the end of each *ThemeWorks* book is a suggestion for a culminating event. In Night Time, for example, the theme study culminates in a pretend campout at school. Each of the events is an outgrowth of many of the theme activities that have gone before. Throughout the theme exploration, children prepare for the culminating event by creating special artwork or construction projects that form the environment of the final event. The culminating event is a good way to end the theme exploration because it gives students a sense of accomplishment, and a chance to show what they know. The children present some of the work they have done, sing the songs they have learned, play some of the games—all within a context relevant to the theme.

At the Seashore

An exploration of the seashore ought to include a trip to the beach, but it need not necessarily be an ocean beach, if you do not live near a coastline. Lake and river beaches have sand, rocks, and pebbles to explore. Shells and other objects found only on ocean beaches can be donated to the class or store-bought for hands-on observation. You may wish to schedule the study of the seashore late in the school year when your day at the beach will likely be warm and sunny.

A Seashore Web

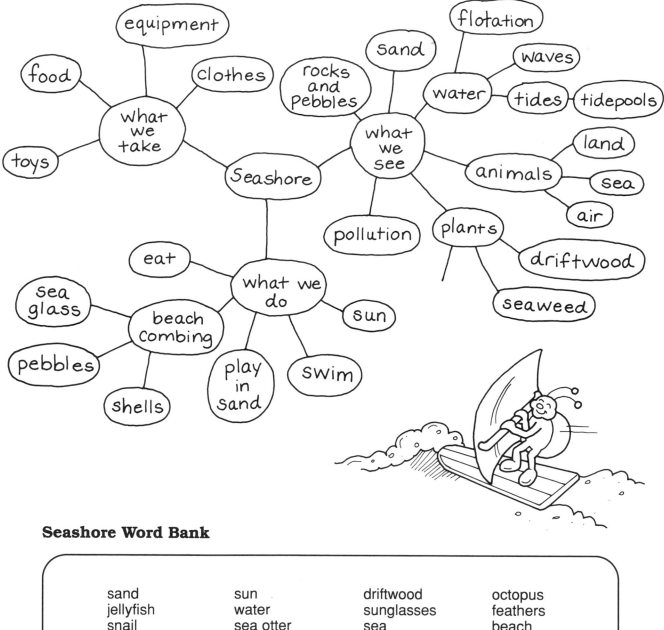

Seashore Word Bank

sand	sun	driftwood	octopus
jellyfish	water	sunglasses	feathers
snail	sea otter	sea	beach
shells	crab	sea gull	waves
pail	pebbles	sea turtle	clam
tide	shovel	rocks	sea horse
pelican	float	beach ball	seaweed
lobster	seal	swim	lighthouse
sea glass	anemone	squid	wade
lifeguard	starfish	fish	sea urchin

THEMEWORKS™ : At the Seashore
©1991 Creative Publications

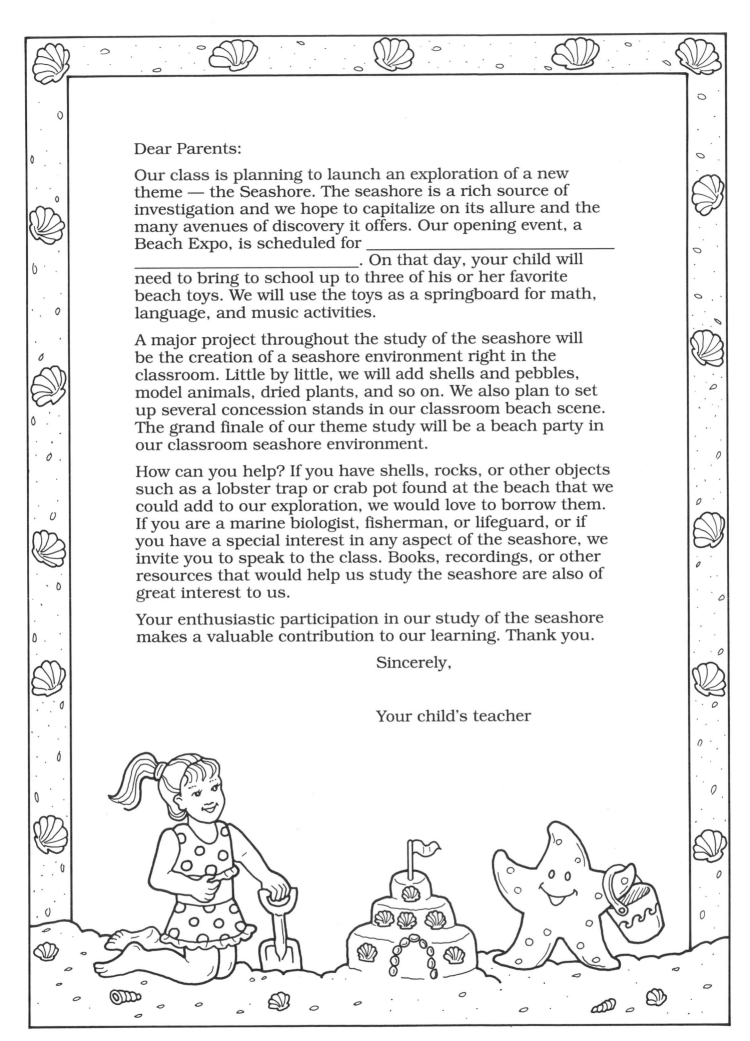

Dear Parents:

Our class is planning to launch an exploration of a new theme — the Seashore. The seashore is a rich source of investigation and we hope to capitalize on its allure and the many avenues of discovery it offers. Our opening event, a Beach Expo, is scheduled for _____ _____. On that day, your child will need to bring to school up to three of his or her favorite beach toys. We will use the toys as a springboard for math, language, and music activities.

A major project throughout the study of the seashore will be the creation of a seashore environment right in the classroom. Little by little, we will add shells and pebbles, model animals, dried plants, and so on. We also plan to set up several concession stands in our classroom beach scene. The grand finale of our theme study will be a beach party in our classroom seashore environment.

How can you help? If you have shells, rocks, or other objects such as a lobster trap or crab pot found at the beach that we could add to our exploration, we would love to borrow them. If you are a marine biologist, fisherman, or lifeguard, or if you have a special interest in any aspect of the seashore, we invite you to speak to the class. Books, recordings, or other resources that would help us study the seashore are also of great interest to us.

Your enthusiastic participation in our study of the seashore makes a valuable contribution to our learning. Thank you.

Sincerely,

Your child's teacher

Our opening event in the study of the Seashore is a Beach Expo, a display of all the kinds of things we like most to take with us to the beach. Children bring from home to share such things as beach balls, sand toys, inflatable water toys, sunglasses, and so on. The beach things are displayed for the day and used as the basis for activities.

Guess My Secret Rule

Secret Rule: Things You Wear to the Beach

Sharing Songs
This is a parody of
Mary Wore a Red Dress.

C
Ben brought his sunglasses,

G7   C
sunglasses, sunglasses.

C
Ben brought his sunglasses,

G7   C
To share with us today.

This song is sung to the tune of the *Farmer in the Dell.*

D
Leslie brought a beach ball.

D
Leslie brought a beach ball.

D   G
Heigh-ho, merry-o,

D   A7
Leslie brought a beach ball.

Both songs can be adapted to describe everyone in the class.

Secret Rule: Things You Take to the Beach.

Other secret rules could be:
    inflatable toys
    things that are red
    things that go in the water

THEMEWORKS™ : At the Seashore
©1991 Creative Publications

Toy Commercials

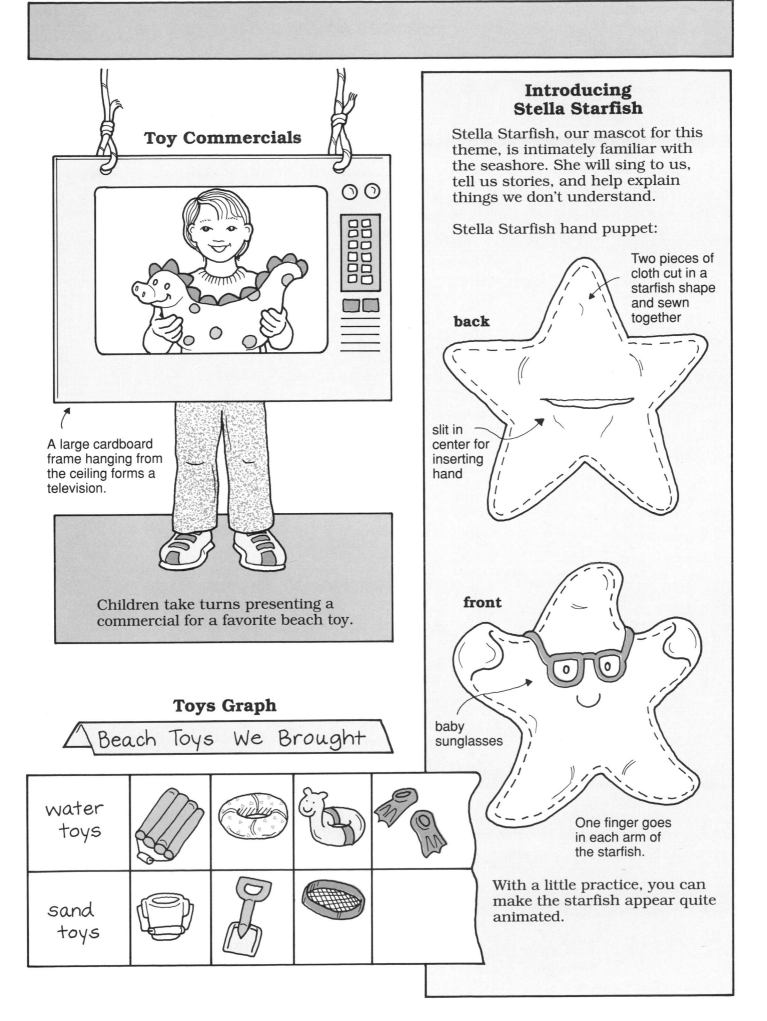

A large cardboard frame hanging from the ceiling forms a television.

Children take turns presenting a commercial for a favorite beach toy.

Introducing Stella Starfish

Stella Starfish, our mascot for this theme, is intimately familiar with the seashore. She will sing to us, tell us stories, and help explain things we don't understand.

Stella Starfish hand puppet:

back

Two pieces of cloth cut in a starfish shape and sewn together

slit in center for inserting hand

front

baby sunglasses

One finger goes in each arm of the starfish.

With a little practice, you can make the starfish appear quite animated.

Toys Graph

Beach Toys We Brought

water toys				
sand toys				

Fun in the Sun

Shore

Play on the seashore
And gather up shells,
Kneel in the damp sands
Digging wells.

Run on the rocks
Where the seaweed slips,
Watch the waves
And the beautiful ships.

Mary Britton Miller

What's Fun in the Sun?

Fun in the sun is:

wading,
floating,
splashing in the water,
building castles,
making rivers,
and getting buried in the sand.

Safety Posters

Fun in the sun can be easily spoiled if care is not taken. The children can share their safety tips through safety posters.

Eva
Don't pick up a jellyfish. They sting.

Joey
Watch the tides.
A big wave may take your things.

Bill
Don't drink sea water. It will make you sick!

Ben
Always swim with a buddy.

Janie
The sun can burn you. Wear suntan lotion.

Tommy
Be careful on rocks. You might slip.

Now's a good time to ask a lifeguard to visit the classroom and tell about safety at the beach.

12

THEMEWORKS™ : At the Seashore
©1991 Creative Publications

Beach Mural

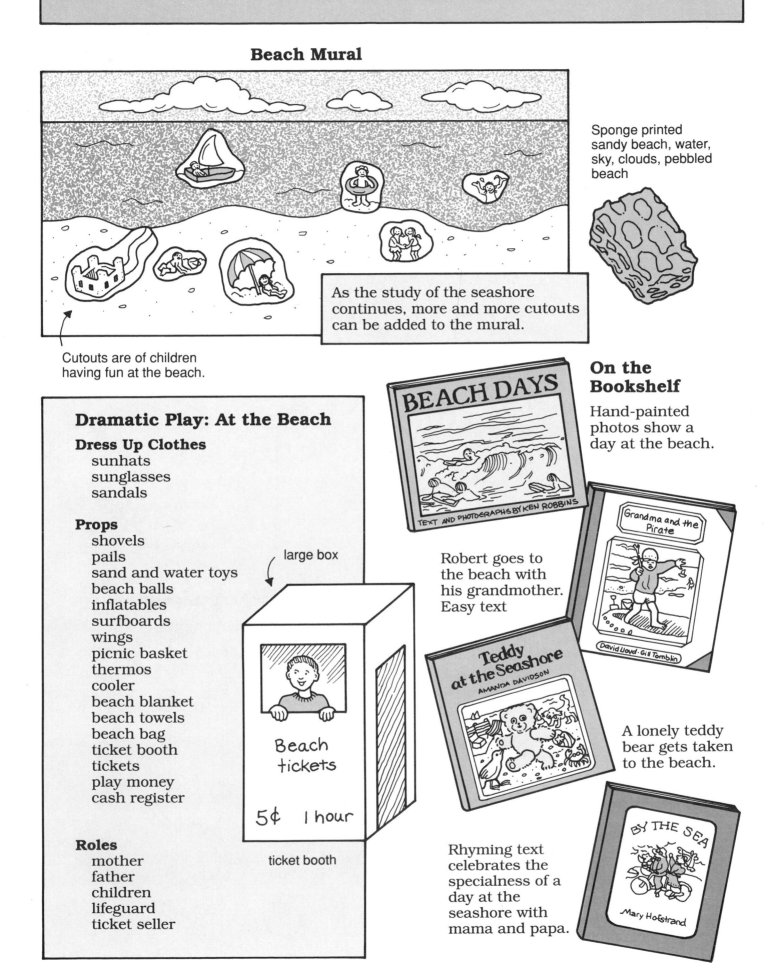

Cutouts are of children having fun at the beach.

Sponge printed sandy beach, water, sky, clouds, pebbled beach

As the study of the seashore continues, more and more cutouts can be added to the mural.

Dramatic Play: At the Beach

Dress Up Clothes
sunhats
sunglasses
sandals

Props
shovels
pails
sand and water toys
beach balls
inflatables
surfboards
wings
picnic basket
thermos
cooler
beach blanket
beach towels
beach bag
ticket booth
tickets
play money
cash register

Roles
mother
father
children
lifeguard
ticket seller

large box

Beach tickets

5¢ 1 hour

ticket booth

On the Bookshelf

Hand-painted photos show a day at the beach.

BEACH DAYS
TEXT AND PHOTOGRAPHS BY KEN ROBBINS

Robert goes to the beach with his grandmother. Easy text

Grandma and the Pirate
David Lloyd · Gill Tomblin

Teddy at the Seashore
AMANDA DAVIDSON

A lonely teddy bear gets taken to the beach.

Rhyming text celebrates the specialness of a day at the seashore with mama and papa.

BY THE SEA
Mary Hofstrand

An Outing to the Beach

If possible, your study of the seashore will include at least one outing to the beach. For a productive day of beachcombing, both the time and the place should be carefully chosen. Not all seashores are suitable for beachcombing. The best time to go is at low tide.

Children should be encouraged to wear old clothes and tennis shoes that can get wet and sandy. A change of clothes can also prove handy, especially on cooler days. Bring plenty of self-closing plastic bags for storing treasures found while beachcombing.

Collection Clubs

The children can be divided into teams. Each team focuses on a different type of beachcombing:

shells
sea glass
pebbles
seaweed
driftwood
feathers

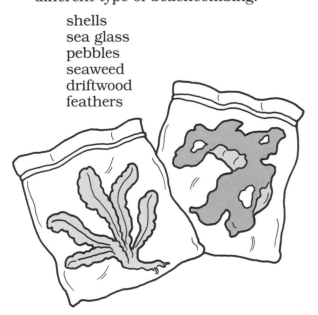

Store each seaweed specimen in a separate plastic bag.

Seashore Sketchpad

Children sketch pictures of things they see at the seashore that they can't take back to the class.

Louisa

We saw a sea otter in the water.

Marcus

We saw sea gulls everywhere.

Taking the Temperature

Temperatures
air   72° F
water   51° F
wet sand
dry sand

THEMEWORKS™ : At the Seashore
©1991 Creative Publications

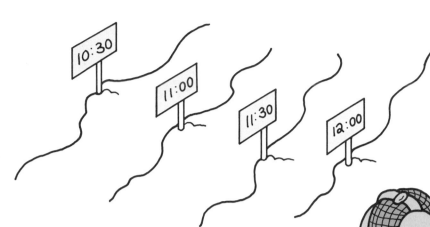

Tide Times

If the tide is going out, children mark the water line at half-hour intervals. If the tide is coming in, the children predict where the tide will be in half-hour intervals.

Signs-of-Life Detectives

Children should be encouraged to look for signs of life at the beach. Tracks in the sand, clam holes, and bubbles all indicate some form of life. Can the children tell what made the track, hole, or bubble?

On the Bookshelf

A story told with the postcards and snapshots sent home to the family.

Postcards

On one side of a 3″ x 5″ card, children draw a picture of something they see at the beach.

Dear Mom and Dad,
We went to the beach.
I saw a pelican dive
into the water.
    Love,
    Lulu

On the other side, they write a short message to their parents telling about their day.

Seashore Sensations

Five Senses Experience Chart

At the Seashore				
I see	I hear	I feel	I smell	I taste
blue water	crashing waves	warm sand	dead fish	salt air
white gulls	barking seals	cold breeze	seaweed	hot dogs
sand dunes	children splashing	hot sun	suntan lotion	lemonade
shiny rocks	people yelling	wet water	barbecue	popsicle
driftwood	seagulls cawing	slippery seaweed		
broken shells	motorboats	cold water		
tiny pebbles	foghorns			

Our Seashore Poetry

Lisa

seaweed
slimy
slippery
stinky
salty

Annie

waves
white caps
crashing
cold and wet

Max

seals
brown and shiny
slippery wet
barking

Starfish...

Lovely poems can come from descriptions of things at the seashore.

THEMEWORKS™ : At the Seashore
©1991 Creative Publications

Sea Gull Song
(to the tune of *Frère Jacques*)

G
I see sea gulls,
G
I see sea gulls,
G   C   D
At the beach,
G   C   D
At the beach,
G
Soaring, diving, fishing,
G
Soaring, diving, fishing,
G   C   D
At the beach,
G   C   D
At the beach.

To learn the song, children repeat each line as a response chant. It can also be sung as a round.

New verses can be created too:
I hear the ocean,
I hear the ocean,
At the beach,
At the beach,
Crashing, splashing, foaming,
Crashing, splashing, foaming,
At the beach,
At the beach.

Sounds of the Seashore

Children can try to identify the different sounds on the tape.

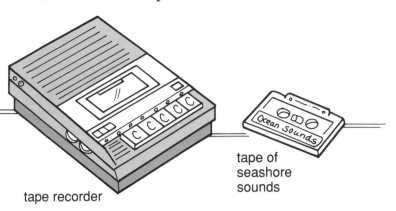

tape recorder

tape of seashore sounds

Driving to the Beach

On the road
smell fumes and tar
through the windows
of the car.

But at the beach
smell suntan lotion
and wind and sun and
ocean!

Joanna Cole

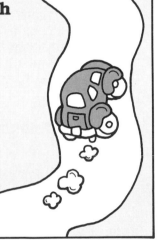

On the Bookshelf

Two children discover the many colors of the sea: sometimes brown as a penny, sometimes as green as a cat's eyes, sometimes even blue.

A dog encounters many different sounds at the seashore. He also discovers some things that don't make sounds.

Photographs show the artistry of nature at the seashore.

Seashore Habitats

Set aside a part of the classroom for a seashore environment.

Habitats:

Sea   Use blue tarp for water.

Sand   Use tan blankets.

Rocks   Use black garbage bags stuffed with crushed newspaper or packing material.

Air   Hang things from the ceiling.

You might want to designate part of the sea as a tide pool area, using rocks to form pools.

Specimens from the seashore field trip, objects such as a lobster trap or crab pot, and any other things donated to the class for study can be displayed in their proper habitats.

Sea, Sand, Rock, and Air

sea	sand	rock	air
fish	crabs	seals	pelicans
sea anemones	sea turtles	crabs	seagulls
starfish	sandpiper	cormorants	
octopus	ice plant		
jellyfish			
snails			
sea urchins			
sea weed			

fish

Two pieces of construction paper form the body. Newspaper is stuffed between the pieces to give the fish a 3-D look.

Seashore Life

Children create models of seashore animals and plants and then place them in their proper habitats.

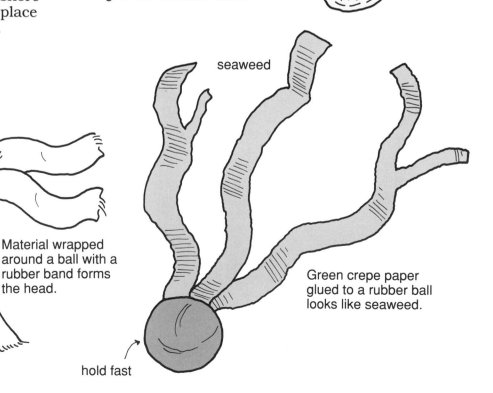

octopus

Material wrapped around a ball with a rubber band forms the head.

The legs are cut from the material below the rubber band.

seaweed

Green crepe paper glued to a rubber ball looks like seaweed.

hold fast

THEMEWORKS™ : At the Seashore
©1991 Creative Publications

Over by the Seashore

(a parody of the rhyme
Over in the Meadow)

1

Over by the seashore
in the sand, in the sun,
Lived an old mother seagull
and her little seagull one.
"Caw," said her mother,
"I caw", said the one.
So they cawed and they cawed
in the sand, in the sun.

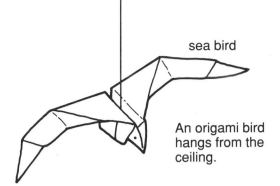

sea bird

An origami bird hangs from the ceiling.

Can You Camouflage?

Children explore camouflage by hiding model animals somewhere in the room where the color of the animal blends in with the things around it. Can classmates find the hidden animals? The animal last found probably has the best camouflage.

2

Over by the seashore
in the water so blue,
Lived an old mother fish
and her little fishies two.
"Swim," said the mother,
"We swim," said the two.
So they swam and they swam
in the water so blue.

snail

A coil of clay was used to make this snail.

3

Over by the seashore
on a rock by the sea,
Lived an old mother seal
and her little pups three.
"Bark", said the mother,
"We bark", said the three.
So they barked and they barked
on a rock by the sea.

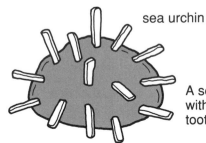

sea urchin

A sea urchin made with clay and toothpicks.

Show It

The children pantomime the activities of seashore animals:

▼ A sea turtle mother swims in the sea. Night comes. The turtle mother crawls slowly to shore and lays her eggs in the warm sand. She buries them with her big flippers so that no one will find them. Then slowly she returns to the sea once again.

Here are some outstanding recordings you can play to accompany the children pantomiming.

▶ A pelican soars above the sea looking for good things to eat. He spots a fish far below and swoops down. Splash, he plunges into the sea and grabs the fish in his huge beak. He carries it to shore where he eats it.

◀ A sea otter floats on her back on the water with her feet pointed to the sky. With a splash, she dives deep down into the sea, picks up some clams and a rock, and returns to float on the sea. She bangs the clams on the rock to break them open and sucks out the meat. Then she cleans her fur with her paw.

20

Seal

See how he dives
  From the rocks with a zoom!
  See how he darts
    Through his watery room
     Past crabs and eels
     And green seaweed,
     Past fluffs of sandy
    Minnow feed!
  See how he swims
    With a swerve and a twist,
  A flip of the flipper,
  A flick of the wrist!
Quicksilver-quick,
  Softer than spray,
Down he plunges
And sweeps away;
Before you can think,
Before you can utter
  Words like "Dill pickle"
Or "Apple butter,"
  Back up he swims
    Past Sting Ray and Shark,
    Out with a zoom,
    A whoop, a bark;
    Before you can say
     Whatever you wish,
      He plops at your side
      With a mouthful of fish!

William Jay Smith

This poem also makes a good source for pantomiming animal actions.

Turtle Poem

This is an adaptation of the poem *The Little Turtle* by Vachel Lindsay.

There was a giant turtle.
He lived in the sea.
He swam in the ocean.
He climbed on the rocks.

He snapped at a mosquito.
He snapped at a flea.
He snapped at a minnow.
And he snapped at me.

He caught the mosquito.
He caught the flea.
He caught the minnow.
But he didn't catch me.

On the Bookshelf

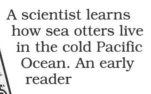

A scientist learns how sea otters live in the cold Pacific Ocean. An early reader

Another early reader, this book documents the life of this fascinating creature of the sea.

The Crab Crawled Over the Sand Dune

Sing to the tune of *The Bear Went Over the Mountain*.

G
The crab crawled over the sand dune,

D   G
The crab crawled over the sand dune,

G   C
The crab crawled over the sand dune,

D   G
To see what he could see.

The other side of the sand dune,
The other side of the sand dune,
The other side of the sand dune,
Was all that he could see.

0 legs — fish

1 leg — flamingo

2 legs — seagull

4 legs — sea turtle

5 legs — starfish

6 legs — fly

8 legs — octopus

10 legs — crab

12 legs — sunstar

The Octopus

Tell me, O Octopus, I begs,
Is those things arms or is they legs?
I marvel at thee, Octopus;
If I were thou, I'd call me Us.

Ogden Nash

Hermit Crabs

Hermit Crabs, which can be bought for pets at some pet stores, are fascinating creatures for children to observe. Like crabs at the seashore, these land animals use empty shells for protection. When they get too big for their present shell, they must move to a larger one. With luck, this will happen one day in your class. Make sure to provide several appropriately sized shell homes for your pet to choose from.

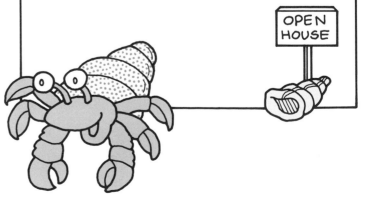

OPEN HOUSE

Now's a perfect time to visit an aquarium or marine world. Or ask a marine biologist to visit the class.

THEMEWORKS™ : At the Seashore
©1991 Creative Publications

What Do You See?

Children enjoy creating variations of Bill Martin Jr.'s book, *Brown Bear, Brown Bear, What Do You See?* Here's the beginning of one for the seashore:

Seagull, seagull what do you see?

I see a purple fish Looking at me.

Purple fish, purple fish, What do you see?

I see a pink crab Looking at me.

Pink crab, pink crab What do you see?

I see a red starfish Looking at me.

The Reason for the Pelican

The reason for the pelican
Is difficult to see:
His beak is clearly larger
Than there's any need to be.

It's not to bail a boat with—
He doesn't own a boat.
Yet everywhere he takes himself
He has that beak to tote.

It's not to keep his wife in—
His wife has got one too.
It's not a scoop for eating soup.
It's not an extra shoe.

It isn't quite for anything.
And yet you realize
It's really quite a splendid beak
In quite a splendid size.

John Ciardi

On the Bookshelf

Friends help a hermit crab decorate a new and bigger shell home. But soon he outgrows it.

A hermit crab searches for a house that fits and will keep him safe from danger.

Obadiah acquires a friend, a sea gull.

Time and Tide Wait for No One

Each day a new sign appears at the classroom beach giving the times for low and high tide. The children watch the clock and signal when low or high tide has arrived. You might want to set the low tide time to correspond with the beginning of a period of time in which you want the children to work on some seashore theme projects.

Today

Low Tide   8:50 a.m.

High Tide   1:30 p.m.

???????????????????????????????????

Question Box

What are tides? Sometimes the water comes far up on the shore. This is called high tide. Sometimes the water does not come up very far. This is low tide. In most places, there are two high tides and two low tides each day.

Why are there tides? The moon has a pull on the Earth, called *gravity*. When the ocean is closest to the moon, its pull is strongest, and the tides are high. When the ocean is farthest from the moon, its pull is less, and the tides are low.

Starfish

The starfish puppet (see page 11) can be used to demonstrate how a starfish breaks open an oyster.

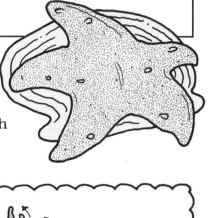

Watercolor Creatures

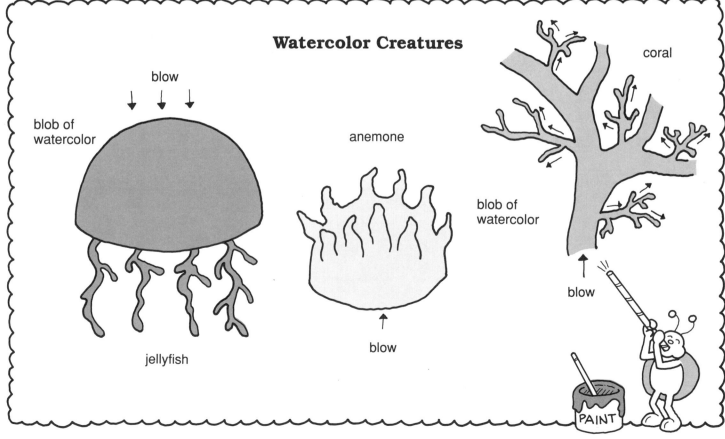

blow

blob of watercolor

jellyfish

anemone

blow

coral

blob of watercolor

blow

PAINT

THEMEWORKS™ : At the Seashore
©1991 Creative Publications

Jellyfish Dance

We use a parachute to create a giant jelly-fish. Crepe paper streamers hanging from the parachute are the jellyfish's tentacles. We open the parachute up as far as it will go, then close it again quickly, mimicking how a jellyfish moves in water.

On the Bookshelf

At the Seafood Market

Visiting a seafood market can be a fascinating experience for young tide pool students. Find a market that has a variety of whole seafoods, such as octopus, squid, shrimp, lobster, mussels, clams, crab. If they're alive, all the better. Children can make drawings of what they see.

Let the children interview the market manager. Questions they might ask:

- Where does the seafood come from?
- When was the seafood caught?
- How was it caught?
- Which kind of seafood do people like best?

If going to a seafood market is out of the question, a whole crab or lobster could be brought to the classroom for the children to examine.

Seafood Tastes

Cook a crab, a lobster, or some shrimp for the children to taste.

The Hungry Waves

The hungry waves along the shore
Chase each other with a roar.

They raise their heads, and wide and high,
Toss their hair against the sky.

They show their teeth in rows of white
And open up their jaws to bite.

Dorothy Aldis

Let the children draw a picture for this poem.

Ocean Wave

In this game, the children slide quickly back and forth, making themselves look like an ocean wave.

To play, everyone sits in chairs arranged in a large circle. One child goes to the center of the circle, and his or her chair is removed. The child calls out, "Slide right" or "Slide left." The seated children move quickly one seat right or left, while the player in the middle tries to grab an empty seat. If he or she succeeds, the child beaten to the chair takes center position.

Slide right!

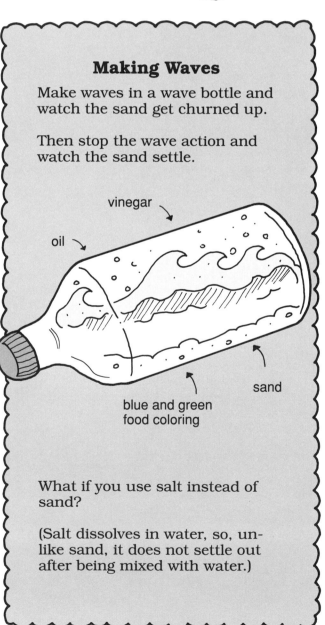

Making Waves

Make waves in a wave bottle and watch the sand get churned up.

Then stop the wave action and watch the sand settle.

vinegar

oil

sand

blue and green food coloring

What if you use salt instead of sand?

(Salt dissolves in water, so, unlike sand, it does not settle out after being mixed with water.)

THEMEWORKS™ : At the Seashore
©1991 Creative Publications

Message in a Bottle

Each day the teacher prepares a different message and sticks it in the bottle. The messages are from people who live across the sea (in Japan or Hawaii, for example). After the message is read to the class, the place where the message originated is found on a globe or wall map.

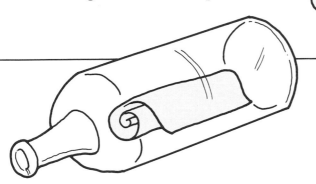

Hello,
My name is Satomi.
I live in Japan. My house is on the

Sea Salt

Water, water everywhere
But not a drop to drink.

How much salt do you think is in a cup of sea water? Predict, then boil sea water to find out.

Caught by a Wave

One group of children forms a long line to represent a wave. The others move toward the wave and take positions as close to the wave as they dare. Then one member of the wave team pulls a number out of a beach pail, and the wave takes that many giant steps forward. The child who is closest to the wave without being caught by it wins. Children who are caught by the wave take the places of members of the wave team. Then the wave returns to the sea, and the game is repeated.

Float or Sink

Children can use the treasures they brought back from the seashore to explore which things float and which things sink. Be sure to include a coconut. Try the message in the bottle too. (See page 27.)

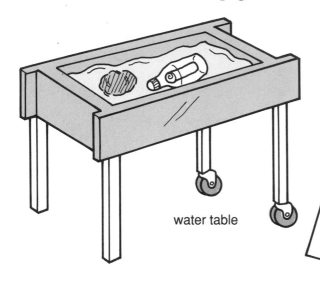

water table

Children can also test beach toys to see if they sink or float. Do most beach toys sink or float? Why?

Beach Toys

Floaters						
Sinkers						

What We Learned

All but one of our beach toys float. If beach toys did not float, we would lose them in the sea.

THEMEWORKS™ : At the Seashore
©1991 Creative Publications

Coconut Boat

In warm sea waters, you may find coconuts along the shores. These giant seeds spread easily to faraway shores because they float. Exploring coconuts is a feast for the senses.

Getting to Know a Coconut

See	Hear	Feel	Smell	Taste
shell hairy round brown monkey-face white meat thin milk	milk sloshing	rough shell strings on shell	milk	milk coconut meat

Coconut Smoothie

Coconut Meat
Coconut Milk
Ice

Blend together until smooth.

Imagine sipping your Coconut Smoothie on a beach in the tropics.

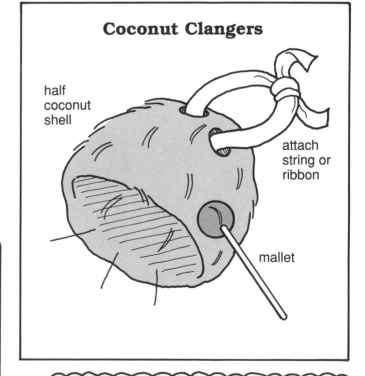

Coconut Clangers

half coconut shell

attach string or ribbon

mallet

Save some Coconut Smoothie for the Beach Party Extravaganza. (See pages 48-51.)

Seashells by the Seashore

Shells for the activities on these pages can be collected at the seashore (see pages 14 to 15), donated by children, parents, or friends of the classroom, or bought in nature stores.

To make a hole in a shell, use a nail and tap it lightly with a hammer.

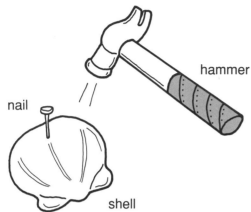

hammer

nail

shell

Seashell Wind Chime

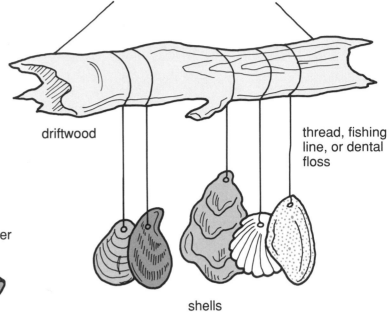

driftwood

thread, fishing line, or dental floss

shells

You may want to experiment with different shells to see which make the best sounds as they clang together in the wind.

Seashell Patterns

Seashell cutouts (see page 52), macaroni shells, or real shells can be used.

adding machine tape

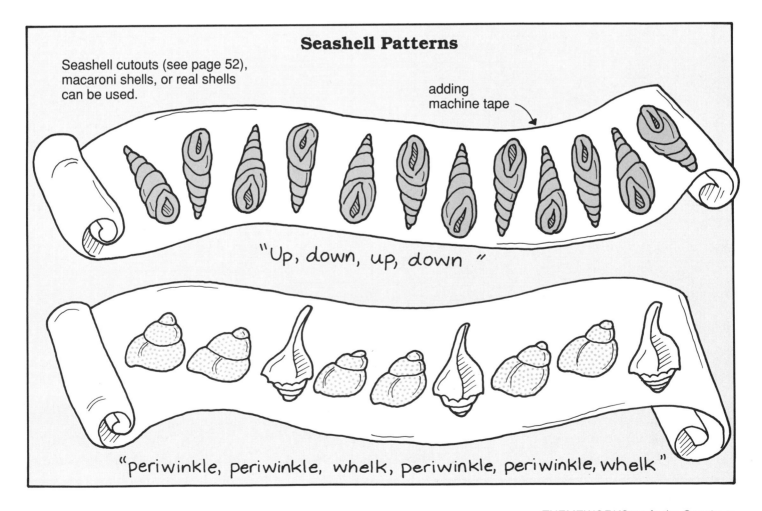

"Up, down, up, down"

"periwinkle, periwinkle, whelk, periwinkle, periwinkle, whelk"

THEMEWORKS™ : At the Seashore
©1991 Creative Publications

I'm Thinking of a Shell

Children take turns describing a shell from a collection of different shells. The others tell which one is being described.

What Is It Like?

My Shell

My shell looks like
a _____ .

I call it a

_____ shell.

Name Matching

Many shells look like their names. Can you match names to these shells?

Names: keyhole limpet
comb murex
heart cockle
leopard cone

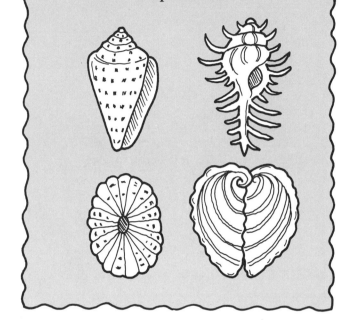

My Shell   Andrew

My shell looks like an ice cream cone.

I call it a cone shell.

My Shell   Fernando

My shell looks like a mountain.

I call it a mountain shell.

My Shell   Heather

My shell looks like an open mouth.

I call it a mouth shell.

Seashell Graph

Shells can be sorted by many different attributes: color, shape, size, design (striped, dotted), type. After many sorting experiences, children can make a graph of their seashell collection:

Shell Estimation

How many more to fill the jar?

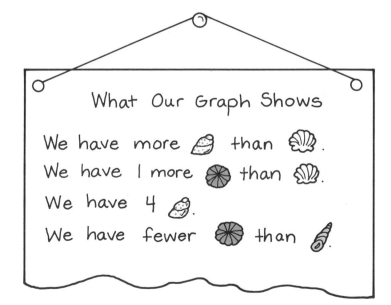

egg cartons

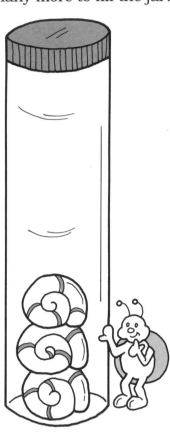

What Our Graph Shows

We have more 🐚 than 🐚.

We have 1 more 🦪 than 🦪.

We have 4 🐚.

We have fewer 🦪 than 🐚.

Question Box

What are shells? The shells we find on the beach were once homes of sea animals that have very soft bodies. The shells protected the sea animals from harm. When the animals died, the shells were left behind. There are two main types of shells. Bivalves have two shells hinged together. Univalves have only one shell.

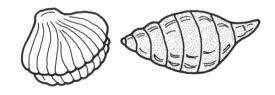

Seashell ID

Even very young children learn from trying to identify shells because the process of comparing a shell to a picture of a shell challenges their powers of observation. To get the most out of the activity, it is best to have the children work in pairs with one shell between them and a shell identification book. Note: Since the goal of the activity is to develop children's observation skills, it is not necessary for them to make an accurate identification.

Seashell Sounds

The sound you hear is actually air going through the shell.

Clam Clackers

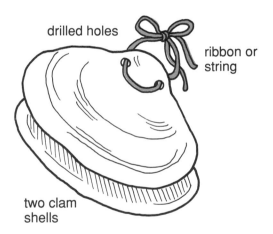

drilled holes

ribbon or string

two clam shells

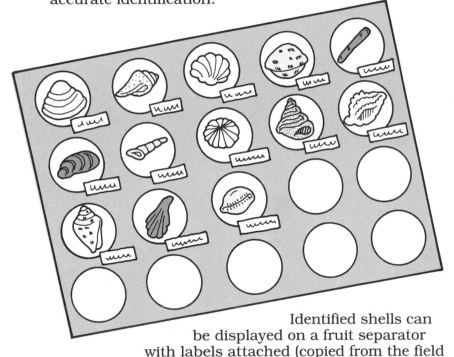

Identified shells can be displayed on a fruit separator with labels attached (copied from the field identification book).

Reference Books

Selling Seashells by the Seashore

Tongue Twisters

We all know the tongue twister "Sally sells seashells by the seashore." But what other tongue twisters can we create?

Teddy
Sandy saw seven sand crabs in the sand.

Kimberly
Stella the starfish stared at the sea.

Timothy
Sailors sail sailing ships over the sea.

Mario
Swimmy swam to the shore in his swimsuit.

Seashore Word Bank

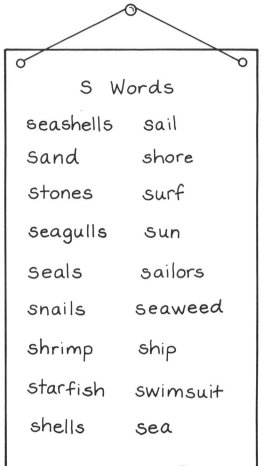

S Words

seashells	sail
sand	shore
stones	surf
seagulls	sun
seals	sailors
snails	seaweed
shrimp	ship
starfish	swimsuit
shells	sea

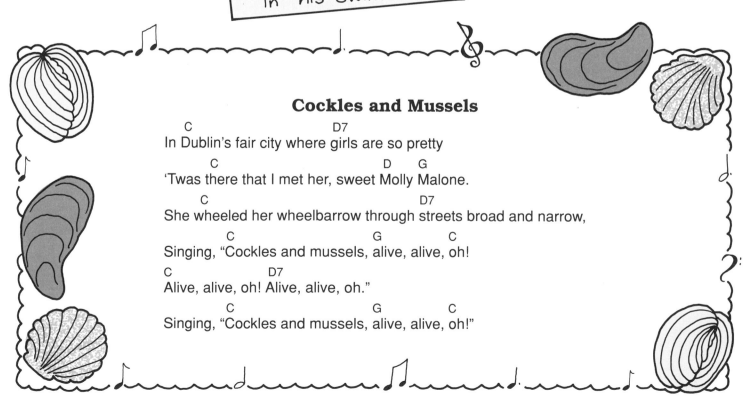

Cockles and Mussels

C   D7
In Dublin's fair city where girls are so pretty

   C   D G
'Twas there that I met her, sweet Molly Malone.

   C   D7
She wheeled her wheelbarrow through streets broad and narrow,

     C   G   C
Singing, "Cockles and mussels, alive, alive, oh!

C   D7
Alive, alive, oh! Alive, alive, oh."

     C   G   C
Singing, "Cockles and mussels, alive, alive, oh!"

THEMEWORKS™ : At the Seashore
©1991 Creative Publications

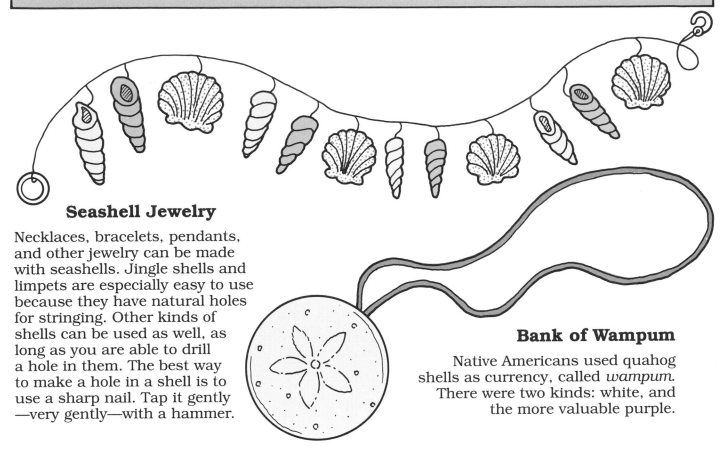

Seashell Jewelry

Necklaces, bracelets, pendants, and other jewelry can be made with seashells. Jingle shells and limpets are especially easy to use because they have natural holes for stringing. Other kinds of shells can be used as well, as long as you are able to drill a hole in them. The best way to make a hole in a shell is to use a sharp nail. Tap it gently —very gently—with a hammer.

Bank of Wampum

Native Americans used quahog shells as currency, called *wampum.* There were two kinds: white, and the more valuable purple.

Jewelry Shop

The jewelry made by the class can be displayed in cases in a seaside jewelry shop.

Box lids lined with velvet or felt fabric help show off the merchandise.

large cardboard box

Pearl's Shell Shoppe

Let the children create their own wampum. Then they can use their new currency to shop at Pearl's Shell Shoppe.

Pebble Paradise

Here are some activities to explore the rocks and pebbles the class found at the beach.

Stone Sorting

Besides color, shape, and size, stones from the seashore can be sorted in innumerable other ways: shiny/dull, smooth/rough, flat/not flat, round/jagged, veined/speckled, holes/no holes.

good for skipping

not good for skipping

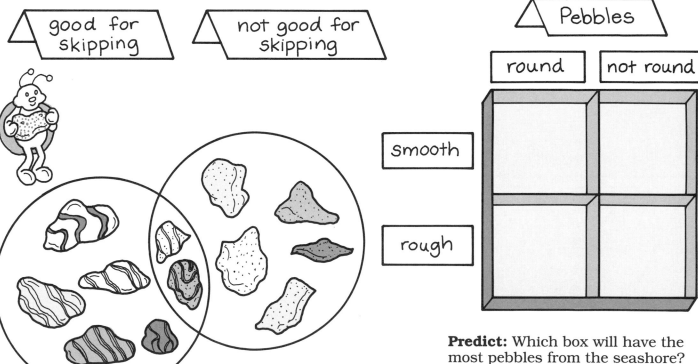

speckled

striped

Rubbing baby oil on the stones adds luster.

Pebble Poets

Pebbles

I see pebbles.

_____ pebbles.

_____ pebbles.

_____ pebbles.

_____ pebbles.

Many kinds of pebbles.

Pebble Matrix

Pebbles

	round	not round
smooth		
rough		

Predict: Which box will have the most pebbles from the seashore? Why?

Most pebbles we find at the seashore have been rubbed smooth by strong sea waves. They have been worn down to a rounded, often flat, shape that makes them easily distinguishable from inland rock.

THEMEWORKS™ : At the Seashore
©1991 Creative Publications

Rock Pets

Felt pen eyes and wings turn ordinary rocks into our favorite seaside animals.

The Black Pebble

There went three children down to the shore,
Down to the shore and back;
There was skipping Susan and bright-eyed Sam
And little scowling Jack.

Susan found a white cockle-shell,
The prettiest ever seen,
And Sam picked up a piece of glass
Rounded and smooth and green.

But Jack found only a plain black pebble
That lay by the rolling sea,
And that was all that ever he found;
So back they went all three.

The cockle-shell they put on the table,
The green glass on the shelf,
But the little black pebble that Jack had found,
He kept it for himself.

James Reeves

Paint by Pebble

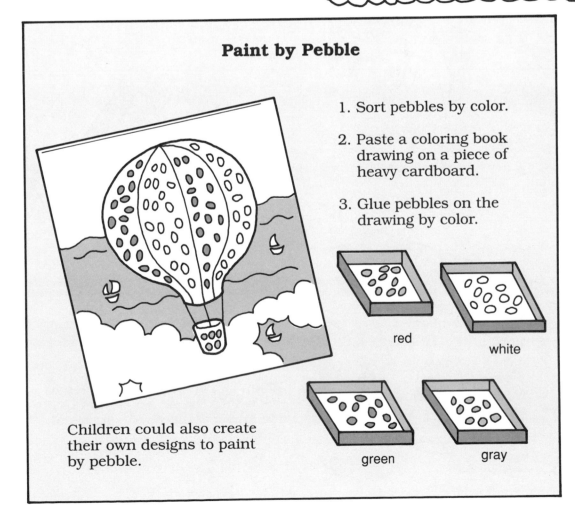

1. Sort pebbles by color.

2. Paste a coloring book drawing on a piece of heavy cardboard.

3. Glue pebbles on the drawing by color.

red

white

green

gray

Children could also create their own designs to paint by pebble.

Pebble Jar

How many rocks do you think are in the jar?

more than 20?
more than 50?
more than 100?

The pebbles in the jar should be fairly uniform in size.

We Built a Castle Near the Rocks

We built a castle near the rocks,
we built it out of sand.

Our fortress was an ice-cream box
with turret, tall and grand.

Our men were twigs, our guns were straws
from which we'd sipped at lunch.

We had the very best of wars...
till someone's foot went CRUNCH!

Joan Walsh Anglund

Sand Casting

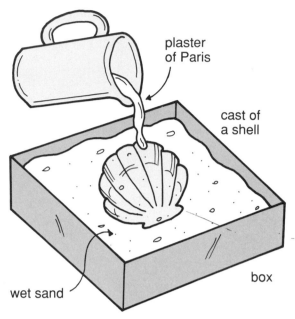

plaster of Paris

cast of a shell

box

wet sand

Our Sand Castle

Sand Making

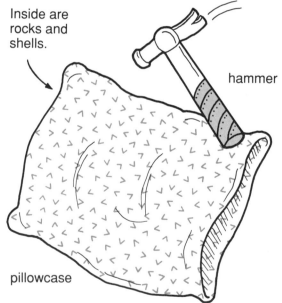

Inside are rocks and shells.

hammer

pillowcase

When you open the pillowcase to see what's inside, you'll find that the smallest pieces are grains of sand.

THEMEWORKS™ : At the Seashore
©1991 Creative Publications

Sand Samples

Children each bring a sample of sand to school. When we look at our sand samples, we discover that sand comes in quite a variety of colors and sizes.

lightest   darkest

We usually think of sand as being white or tan, but on some beaches in Hawaii, the sand is black.

Sand Shakers

toilet
paper roll

sand inside

paper circles
glued to ends

pencil

Sand Paintings

You can use the sand samples. Or you might want to mix food coloring with the sand to create more vibrant colors for the sand paintings.

1. Draw a design with glue on cardboard.

2. Sprinkle sand of different colors on the glue.

3. Pour off excess sand into a tray.

On the Bookshelf

A child's building of a mountain in the sand at the beach is compared to the way a mountain comes to be.

Seashore Celebration

Sing a Song of the Seashore

We changed the underlined words from the rhyme *Sing a Song of Sixpence* to create this jingle about the seashore.

Sing a song of <u>the seashore</u>.
A pocketful of <u>shells</u>.
Four and twenty <u>seagulls</u>.
Asleep in a mudpie.

When the pie was open,
The birds began to sing.
Wasn't that a dainty dish
To set before the <u>children</u>?

The boy was in <u>the ocean</u>
<u>Swimming back and forth</u>.
The girl was <u>on the beach</u>
<u>Playing in the sand</u>.

The baby was in <u>her cradle</u>,
Eating <u>hot dogs and chips</u>,
When along came a <u>seagull</u>
And kissed her pretty nose.

On the Bookshelf

SEA SUMS
by Samuel French Morse
Illus. by Fuku Akino

Counting things at the beach to ten, then back to zero again as the fog rolls in.

Seashore Rhymes

shell	sand	sea	rock
bell	band	be	lock
well	and	we	knock
tell	hand	he	sock
fell	brand	me	shock
knell	land	knee	block
sell	stand	key	clock
spell		tree	
yell		see	

THEMEWORKS™ : At the Seashore
©1991 Creative Publications

The Foghorn: A Playground Game

A few children are foghorns. They station themselves close to playground equipment that the ships are to avoid. They blow foghorns made of construction paper. The rest of the children are ships on a foggy night. Each of the ships is blindfolded and must find its way through the playground without bumping into the playground equipment.

foghorn

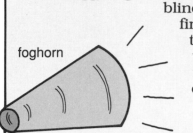

I'd Like to Be a Lighthouse

I'd like to be a lighthouse
    And scrubbed and painted white.
I'd like to be a lighthouse
    And stay awake all night.
To keep my eye on everything
    That sails my patch of sea;
I'd like to be a lighthouse
    With the ships all watching me.

Rachel Field

Model Lighthouse

clear plastic cup

cutout window for access to flashlight's on/off switch

flashlight covered with construction paper

matchbox house with cardboard roof

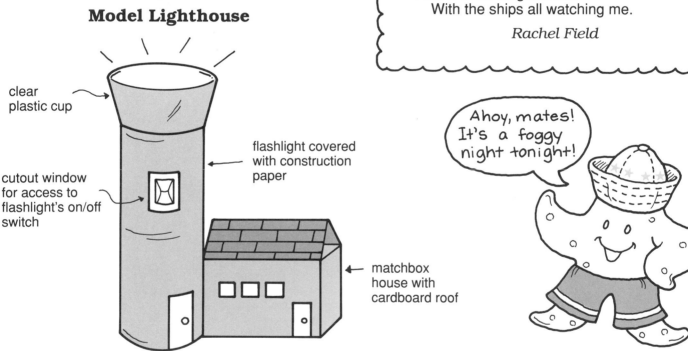

I'd Like to Be

Kimiko — I'd like to be an octopus And have 8 arms.

Juan — I'd like to be a seagull And fly above the water all day.

Isabella — I'd like to be a sea otter And float on my back on the water and play.

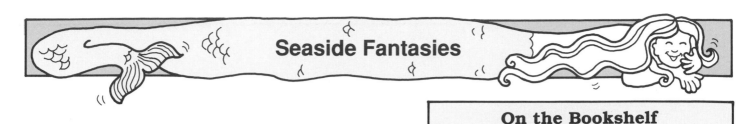
Little Mermaids and Little Mermen

The most enduring seaside fantasy is that of the mermaid, a creature whose upper body and head are that of a woman and whose lower body is the tail of a fish. Mermen are, of course, male mermaids.

Monster Making

Fancy clothes and monster masks turn the children into sea monsters.

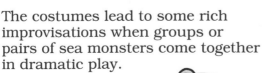

The costumes lead to some rich improvisations when groups or pairs of sea monsters come together in dramatic play.

Some groups might enjoy putting on a skit for the rest of the class.

On the Bookshelf

A fisherman saves a turtle, who then takes him to a fantastic world under the sea.

Miss Moody opens a bottle that says "Do Not Open," and a terrible monster emerges.

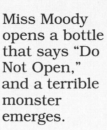

Shirley's imagination takes her far away from what's really happening on the beach.

Kermit is a selfish hermit crab that hoards things he finds on the beach.

Harry gets covered with seaweed, and everyone thinks he is a sea monster.

THEMEWORKS™ : At the Seashore
©1991 Creative Publications

Treasure Chests

Small metal or wooden boxes make good treasure chests. Or cardboard boxes can be painted to look like treasure chests. The treasure chests can be filled with "gold doubloons" (pennies).

Jane, Meg, Mary

We thought there must be about 100 in the chest. But there were only 57.

Scary Sea Creatures

Mermaids and sea serpents are make-believe sea creatures. But some real sea creatures are equally exotic, even scary.

Scary Sea Creatures

octopus

jellyfish

squid

lobsters

sharks

walrus

Who's Afraid?

Who's afraid of an octopus?

afraid					
not afraid					

Nature or Not?

natural	not natural
shells	sea glass
sand	styrofoam
pebbles	plastic
driftwood	bottles
seaweed	cans
feathers	oil
plants	

Oil Spill in a Bottle

clear bottle

3 cups water

½ cup oil

a few drops of blue food coloring

Some questions to explore:

• What happens when you shake the bottle?

• Does oil dissolve in water?

• If you let the bottle sit for a while, where does the oil settle?

Oil Art

1. Fill a shallow pan half full of water.

2. Make oil paint by mixing cooking oil and powder paint.

3. Pour a few drops of oil paint in the pan.

4. Lay a sheet of paper over the water for a few minutes to catch the oil.

5. Lay the paper flat to dry.

THEMEWORKS™ : At the Seashore
©1991 Creative Publications

Sea Glass Graph

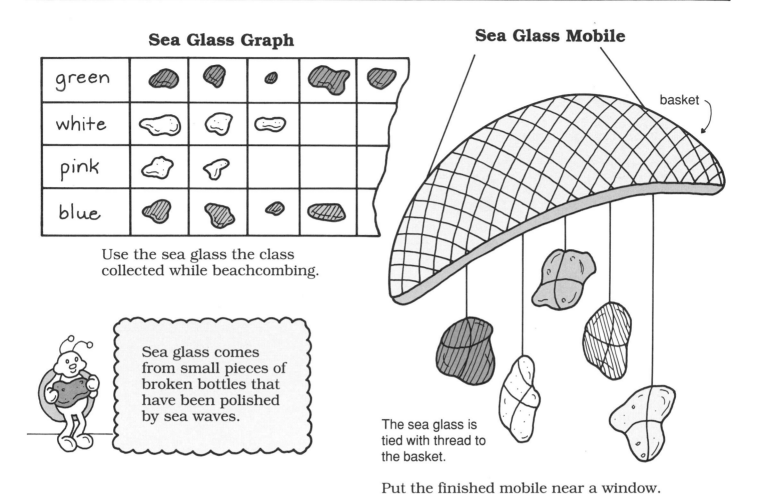

Use the sea glass the class collected while beachcombing.

Sea glass comes from small pieces of broken bottles that have been polished by sea waves.

Sea Glass Mobile

basket

The sea glass is tied with thread to the basket.

Put the finished mobile near a window.

Pollution Posters

Rachel

Throw away your trash.

trash

Paul

Starfish says

Keep the beaches clean!

Helping Birds Fly Free

Help keep our animals safe.

The plastic rings that hold six-packs of cans together are dangerous to birds and fish when they get into the environment. Show children how to cut the rings or pull them apart before throwing them away. Children can make a significant personal contribution to a safer environment with this small act.

Seaside Fast Food

We set up concession stands on the classroom beach in preparation for the Beach Party Extravaganza. (See pages 48 to 51.)

Lemonade Stand

Lemonade 5¢

large box for a stand

Lemonade

10 lemons
7 cups water
1 cup sugar
ice

Squeeze the lemons. Mix the lemon juice, water, and sugar in a large pitcher. Add ice.

Hot Dog Stand

Heat the hot dogs in a hot pot.

Hot Dogs $2

Sales Figures

1		5¢
2		10¢
3		15¢
4		20¢
5		25¢
6		30¢

Dog Sales

1		$2
2		$4
3		$6
4		$8
5		$10
6		$12

THEMEWORKS™ : At the Seashore
©1991 Creative Publications

Snack Packs

Fish crackers make a nice snack. Sell them in bags of ten.

FISH CRACKERS   FISH CRACKERS

Snack Packs   Jeff, Linda, Sam

We put 10 fish in each bag. We made 8 bags. There were two more fish. That's not enough for another bag. There are 82 fish in all.

10 20 30 40 50 60 70 80 81 82

Bag o' Fish

Snack Packs   10¢

Snack Sales

1	2	3	4	5
10¢	20¢	30¢	40¢	5(

Ad Campaign

SMACKING GOOD   Lemonade

Bag o' fish Can't stop eating them

On the Bookshelf

SAND CAKE   A FRANK ASCH Bear Story

Papa Bear makes a cake by drawing ingredients in the sand.

Beach Party Extravaganza

This is the culminating event in our study of the Seashore. The Beach Party Extravaganza takes place at the classroom seashore we've been creating over the last few weeks. Ocean sound tapes provide an aural background to our pretend day at the beach. At the party, we sing sea chanteys, play our seashore instruments, tell yarns, go for a treasure hunt, and use gold doubloons (see page 43) to buy food at our Seaside Food Stands (see pages 46-47).

driftwood board sign

THEMEWORKS™ : At the Seashore
©1991 Creative Publications

Treasure Map

The map shows where to find a treasure chest in the classroom seashore environment.

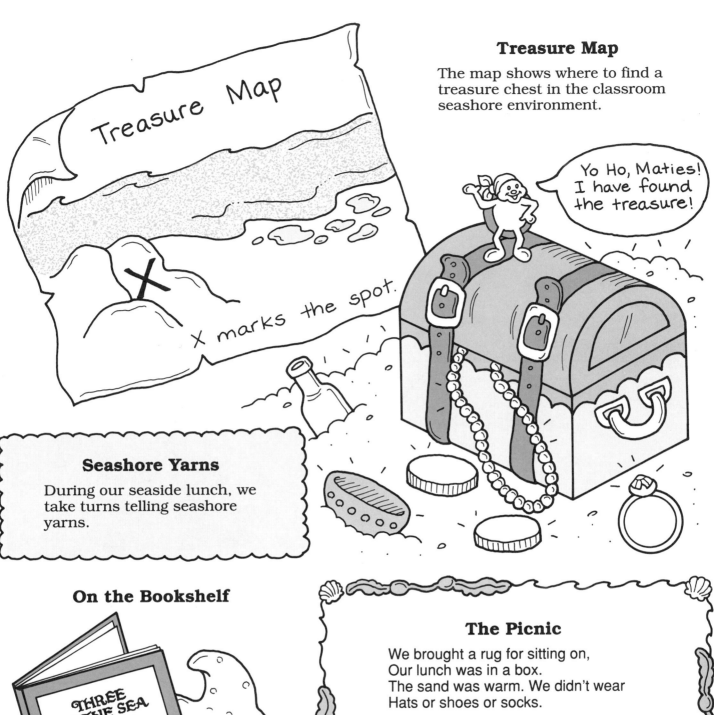

Seashore Yarns

During our seaside lunch, we take turns telling seashore yarns.

On the Bookshelf

Three friends relax after their picnic lunch by telling their best stories. An early reader

The Picnic

We brought a rug for sitting on,
Our lunch was in a box.
The sand was warm. We didn't wear
Hats or shoes or socks.

Waves came curling up the beach.
We waded. It was fun.
Our sandwiches were different kinds.
I dropped my jelly one.

Dorothy Aldis

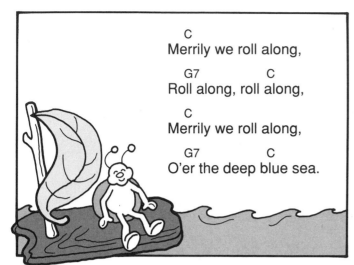

C
Merrily we roll along,

G7   C
Roll along, roll along,

C
Merrily we roll along,

G7   C
O'er the deep blue sea.

D   A7
There's a hole in the bottom of the sea.

A7   D
There's a hole in the bottom of the sea.

G
There's a hole, there's a hole,

D
There's a hole, there's a hole,

A7   D
There's a hole in the bottom of the sea.

Charlie over the ocean,

Charlie over the sea,

Charlie caught a blackbird,

But he can't catch me.

Variations of this chant can be created for each of the children in the class. Just change the name, the verb *caught*, and the object. Examples:

Lester over the ocean,

Lester over the sea,

Lester found a seashell,

But he can't find me.

Tanya over the ocean,

Tanya over the sea,

Tanya saw a pelican,

But she can't see me.

THEMEWORKS™ : At the Seashore
©1991 Creative Publications

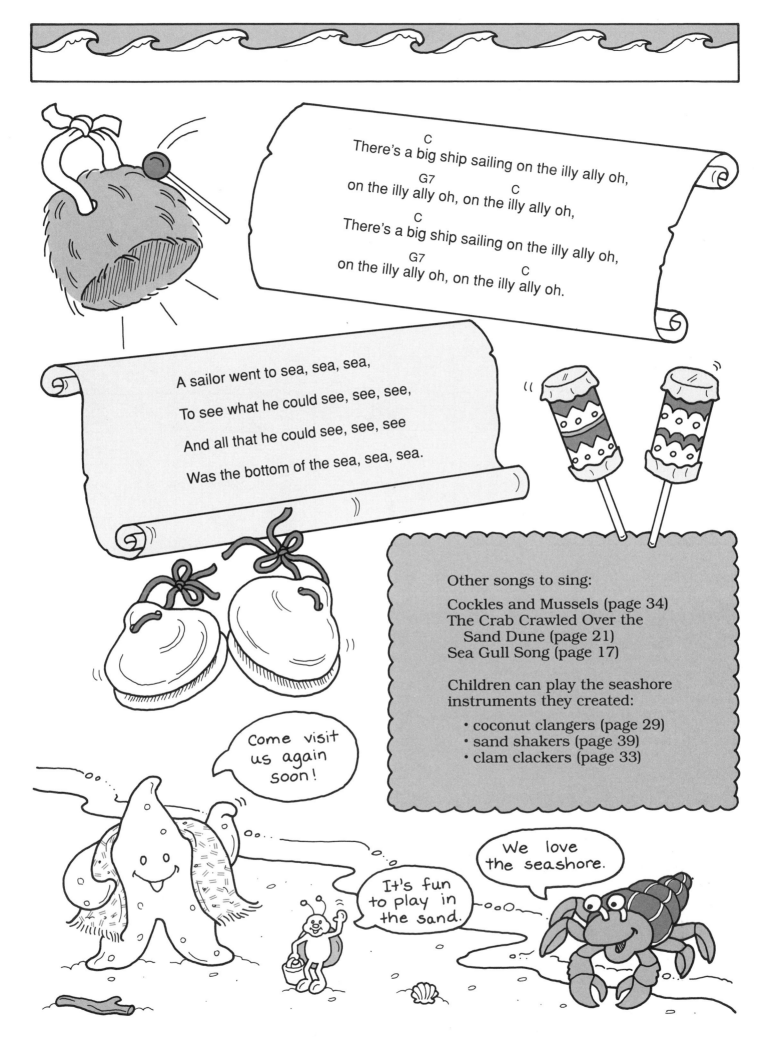

There's a big ship sailing on the illy ally oh,
on the illy ally oh, on the illy ally oh,
There's a big ship sailing on the illy ally oh,
on the illy ally oh, on the illy ally oh.

A sailor went to sea, sea, sea,

To see what he could see, see, see,

And all that he could see, see, see

Was the bottom of the sea, sea, sea.

Other songs to sing:

Cockles and Mussels (page 34)
The Crab Crawled Over the
    Sand Dune (page 21)
Sea Gull Song (page 17)

Children can play the seashore
instruments they created:

• coconut clangers (page 29)
• sand shakers (page 39)
• clam clackers (page 33)

Come visit us again soon!

It's fun to play in the sand.

We love the seashore.

Seashell Pattern Cards

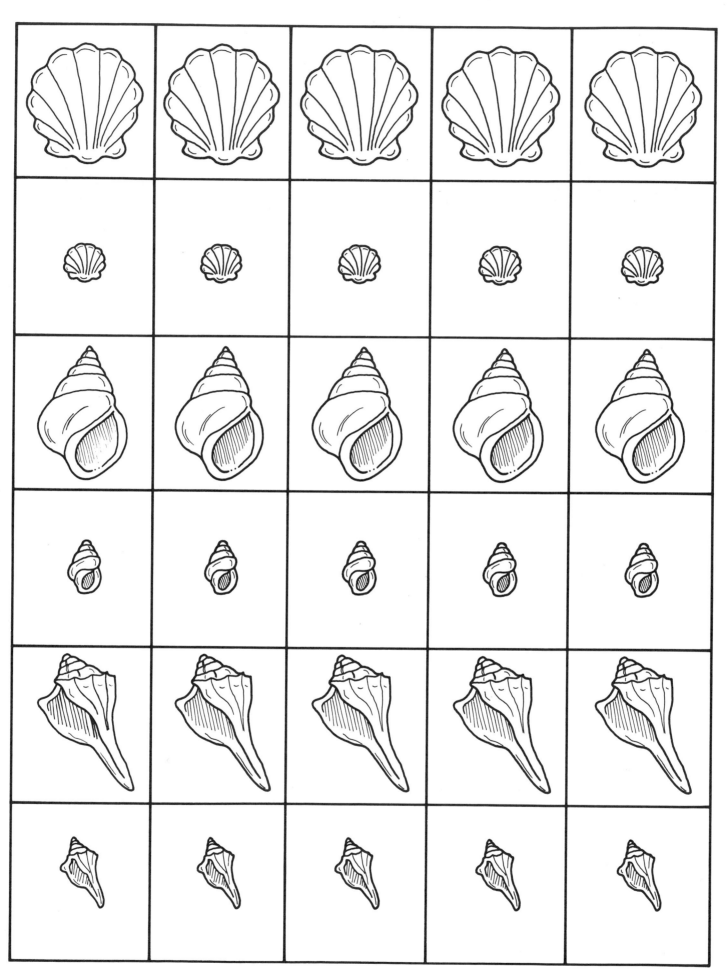

Picture Cards

jellyfish

sea otter

sea gull

clam

pelican

seal

fish

octopus

snail

THEMEWORKS™ : At the Seashore

Picture Cards

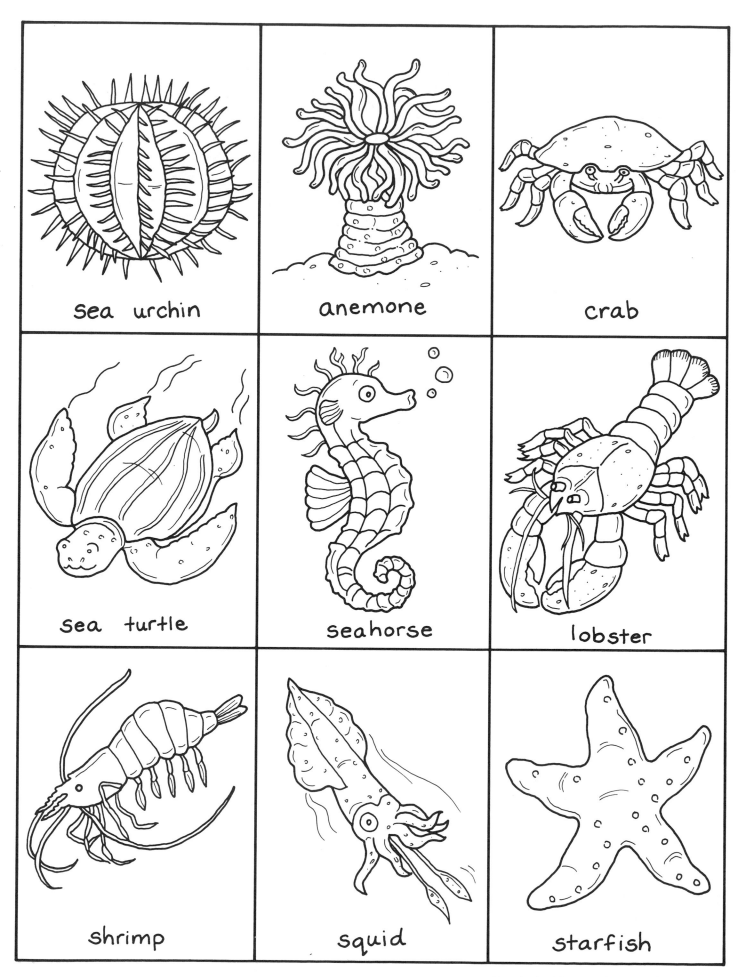

sea urchin

anemone

crab

sea turtle

seahorse

lobster

shrimp

squid

starfish

Picture Cards

sun

sunglasses

lighthouse

pail

shovel

beach ball

shell

seaweed

feather

Word Cards

beach	sand	sea
pail	shovel	beach ball
wave	tide	water
float	wade	swim
shell	pebble	rock
sun	feather	driftwood
clam	starfish	seal
fish	snail	crab

THEMEWORKS™ : At the Seashore
©1991 Creative Publications

At the Seashore

THEMEWORKS™ : At the Seashore

Curriculum Chart

	Language	Mathematics	Science	Social Studies	Art	Cooking	Music/Movement	P.E.	Dramatic Play
Beach Expo pp. 10 - 11	• commercials	• classifying • graphing					• song		
Fun in the Sun pp. 12 - 13	• poem • group writing • posters • storybooks • interview	• money • time	• health and safety	• family roles • occupations	• mural • sponge printing • drawing				• day at the beach
Beach-combers All pp. 14 - 15	• picture captions • postcards • storybook	• temperature • time	• field study • tides	• signs of life	• sketching nature • postcards				
Seashore Sensations pp. 16 - 17	• storybooks • poem • experience chart • writing poems • new verses		• five senses • sound ID		• drawing		• song		
What Goes Where? pp. 18 - 19	• rhyme parody	• classifying	• animals and plants • camouflage	• habitats	• 3-D models				

Curriculum Chart

	Language	Mathematics	Science	Social Studies	Art	Cooking	Music/Movement	P.E.	Dramatic Play
Animal Actions pp. 20 - 21	• oral vocab: action verbs • poems • storybooks		• animal movement				• song	• pantomime	
Seashore Potpourri pp. 22 - 23	• poems • chant • storybooks	• number	• seashore animals		• drawings				
The Tide Is Out pp. 24 - 25	• reading signs • storybooks • interview	• time	• tides • animal life	• occupations	• watercolor creatures • drawings	• seafood		• jellyfish dance	• puppet
Catching the Waves pp. 26 - 27	• poem	• measurement • number	• wave action • sea salt	• faraway lands and people	• drawing			• indoor game • outdoor game	
Floating Away pp. 28 - 29	• reading • experience chart	• measurement • graph	• float or sink • five senses			• coconut drink	• coconut clangers		

Curriculum Chart

	Language	Mathematics	Science	Social Studies	Art	Cooking	Music/Movement	P.E.	Dramatic Play
Seashells by the Seashore pp. 30 - 31	• oral descriptions • similes • frame writing	• patterns	• sounds • shells		• drawing		• wind chimes		
Shells and More Shells pp. 32 - 33	• labels	• graph • estimation	• shell ID • sounds						
Selling Seashells pp. 34 - 35	• tongue twisters • phonics	• patterns • money	• shells	• Native American culture • economics	• jewelry making • drawing		• song		
Pebble Paradise pp. 36 - 37	• language frame • poem	• estimation • sorting • matrix classification	• rocks		• rock sculptures • rock mosaics				
Sand Study pp. 38 - 39	• poem	• geometric shapes	• sand making • sand samples • geology	• castles	• sand paintings • sandcasting • construction		• sand shakers		• story acting

THEMEWORKS™ : At the Seashore
©1991 Creative Publications

Curriculum Chart

	Language	Mathematics	Science	Social Studies	Art	Cooking	Music/Movement	P.E.	Dramatic Play
Seashore Celebration pp. 40 - 41	• writing • mother goose parody • rhyming words • poems	• graph • counting	• sounds	• signals	• drawing • construction			• foghorn game	
Seaside Fantasies pp. 42 - 43	• storybooks • brainstorming	• estimation • place value • survey • graph	• sea creatures	• folklore • reality vs. fantasy	• costumes • masks				• sea fantasies
Pollution Solution pp. 44 - 45	• poster • experience chart	• graph • counting back	• oil and water experiments	• pollution • natural vs. manmade	• mobile • poster		• song		
Seaside Fast Food pp. 46 - 47	• advertisement • storybook	• measurement • number • money • function tables • place value		• economics	• drawings for ads	• lemonade • hot dogs			• store
Beach Party Extravaganza pp. 48 - 51	• telling yarns • chants • storybook • poem	• money	• sounds of the sea	• treasure map			• songs • instruments		• beach party

Resource List

Stories

Asch, Frank. *Sand Cake*. New York: Parents' Magazine Press, 1978.

Atwood, Ann. *New Moon Cove*. New York: Scribner's, 1969.

Brown, Margaret Wise. *The Seashore Noisy Book*. New York: Harper and Row, 1941.

Burningham, John. *Come Away from the Water, Shirley*. New York: Thomas Y. Crowell, 1977.

Cole, Sheila. *When the Tide is Low*. New York: Lothrop, Lee and Shepard, 1985.

Carle, Eric. *A House for Hermit Crab*. Saxonville, MA: Picture Book Studio, 1987.

Davidson, Amanda. *Teddy at the Seashore*. New York: Holt, Rinehart and Winston, 1984.

Hofstrand, Mary. *By the Sea*. New York: Viking Press, 1990.

Lloyd, David. *Grandma and the Pirate*. New York: Crown, 1985.

Lund, Doris Herald. *The Paint-Box Sea*. New York: McGraw-Hill, 1973.

Marshall, Edward. *Three by the Sea*. New York: Dial, 1981.

McDonald, Megan. *Is This a House for a Hermit Crab?* Granville, OH: Orchard, 1990.

Morris, Robert A. *Seahorse*. New York: Harper and Row, 1972.

Morse, Samuel French. *Sea Sums*. Boston: Little, Brown, 1970.

Peet, Bill. *Kermit the Hermit*. Boston: Houghton Mifflin, 1965.

Peters, Lisa W. *The Sun, the Wind, and the Rain*. New York: Henry Holt, 1988.

Robbins, Ken. *Beach Days*. New York: Viking Press, 1987.

Shaw, Evelyn. *Sea Otters*. New York: Harper and Row, 1980.

THEMEWORKS™ : At the Seashore
©1991 Creative Publications

Turkle, Brinton. *Do Not Open.* New York: E.P. Dutton, 1981.

Williams, Vera B. *Stringbean's Trip to the Shining Sea.* New York: Greenwillow Books, 1988.

Yashima, Taro. *Seashore Story.* New York: Viking Press, 1967.

Zion, Gene. *Harry by the Sea.* New York: Harper and Row, 1965.

Nonfiction

Florian, Douglas. *Discovering Seashells.* New York: Scribner's. 1986.

Malnig, Anita. *Where the Waves Break: Life at the Edge of the Sea.* Minneapolis: Carolrhoda Books, 1985.

Oxford Scientific Films. *Jellyfish and Other Sea Creatures.* New York: Putnam, 1981.

Selsam, Millicent E. and Hunt, Joyce. *A First Look at Seashells.* New York: Walker, 1983.

Tucker, Abbott. *Seashells of the World.* New York: Western Publishing Co., 1962.

Songs

Cockles and Mussels

Merrily We Roll Along

There's a Hole in the Bottom of the Sea

Recordings

Ocean sounds tape

La Mer by Claude Debussy

Sea Symphony by Ralph Vaughan Williams

Acknowledgements

Grateful acknowledgement is made to the following for permission to reprint their copyrighted material. Every reasonable effort has been made to trace the ownership of all copyrighted material included in this book. Any errors which may have occurred are inadvertent and will be corrected in subsequent editions, provided notification is sent to the publisher.

Dorothy Aldis "The Picnic" from ALL TOGETHER. Copyright © 1925-1928, renewed 1953-1956, 1962, 1967 by Dorothy Aldis. Reprinted by permission of G. P. Putnam's Sons.

Dorothy Aldis "The Hungry Waves" from HERE, THERE, AND EVERYWHERE by Dorothy Aldis. Copyright © 1927, 1928, renewed 1955, 1956 by Dorothy Aldis. Reprinted by permission of G. P. Putnam's Sons.

Joan Walsh Anglund "We Built a Castle Near the Rocks" from MORNING IS A LITTLE CHILD Copyright © 1969 by Joan Walsh Anglund. Reprinted by permission of Harcourt Brace Jovanovich, Inc.

John Ciardi "The Reason for the Pelican" from THE REASON FOR THE PELICAN Copyright © 1955 Curtis Publishing Co.. Published by J. B. Lippincott Company. Reprinted by permission of Mrs. Judith H. Ciardi.

Joanna Cole "Driving to the Beach" Copyright © 1973 by Joanna Cole. Reprinted by permission of Joanna Cole.

Rachel Field "I'd Like to Be a Lighthouse" from TAXIS AND TOADSTOOLS by Rachel Field. Copyright © 1926 by Doubleday, a division of Bantam, Doubleday, Dell Publishing Group, Inc. Used by permission of the publisher.

Mary Britton Miller "Shore" from MENAGERIE by Mary Britton Miller, Macmillan Publishing Co. Reprinted by permission of the estate of Mary Britton Miller.

Ogden Nash "The Octopus" from VERSES FROM 1929 ON by Ogden Nash. Copyright © 1942 Ogden Nash. Used by permission of Little, Brown and Co.

James Reeves "The Black Pebble" from WANDERING MOON AND OTHER POEMS by James Reeves, Puffin Books. Copyright by James Reeves. Reprinted by permission of The James Reeves Estate.

William Jay Smith "Seal" from LAUGHING TIME by William Jay Smith. Copyright © 1955, 1957, 1980, 1990 by William Jay Smith. Reprinted by permission of Farrar, Straus and Giroux, Inc.